Take Care of Yourself

Eating Well

Siân Smith

www.raintreepublishers.co.uk
Visit our website to find out
more information about
Raintree books.

To order:
☎ Phone 0845 6044371
🖷 Fax +44 (0) 1865 312263
🖳 Email myorders@raintreepublishers.co.uk

Customers from outside the UK please telephone +44 1865 312262

Raintree is an imprint of Capstone Global Library Limited,
a company incorporated in England and Wales having its
registered office at 7 Pilgrim Street, London, EC4V 6LB –
Registered company number: 6695582

Edited by Dan Nunn, Rebecca Rissman,
  and John-Paul Wilkins
Designed by Victoria Allen
Picture research by Tracy Cummins
Production by Alison Parsons
Originated by Capstone Global Library Ltd
Printed and bound in China by Leo Paper Products Ltd

ISBN 978 1 406 24161 7 (hardback)
16 15 14 13 12
10 9 8 7 6 5 4 3 2 1

ISBN 978 1 406 24168 6 (paperback)
17 16 15
10 9 8 7 6 5 4 3 2

British Library Cataloguing in Publication Data
Smith, Siân.
Eating well. -- (Take care of yourself)
613.2-dc22
A full catalogue record of this book is available from the
British Library.

Acknowledgements
We would like to thank the following for permission to
reproduce photographs: Capstone Publishers pp. 9, 13 inset,
19 (Karon Dubke); Food.gov.uk p. 5 (©Crowncopyright2011);
Getty Images pp. 8, 20 (Digital Vision), 12 (Sven Schrader),
13 (JGI/Jamie Grill); istockphoto pp. 7 (© Aldo Murillo), 11
(© Dmitriy Shironosov), 15, 23b (© Christopher Futcher);
Shutterstock pp. 4 (© Monkey Business Images), 6 (© spotmatik),
10, 23a (© yamix), 14, 23c (© Jo Mikus), 16 (© Nitr), 17 (©
highviews), 18 (© Shestakoff), 21 (© Forster Forest), 22a (©
Feng Yu), 22b (© Nayashkova Olga), 22c (© Yasonya), 22d (©
Picsfive).

Front cover photograph of boy eating watermelon wedge
reproduced with permission of Getty Images (Jupiterimages).
Rear cover photograph of children eating reproduced with
permission of Shutterstock Images (© Monkey Business Images).

Every effort has been made to contact copyright holders of
material reproduced in this book. Any omissions will be rectified
in subsequent printings if notice is given to the publisher.

We would like to thank Nancy Harris and Dee Reid for their
assistance in the preparation of this book.

Contents

Eating well

When you eat well you give
your body the food it needs.

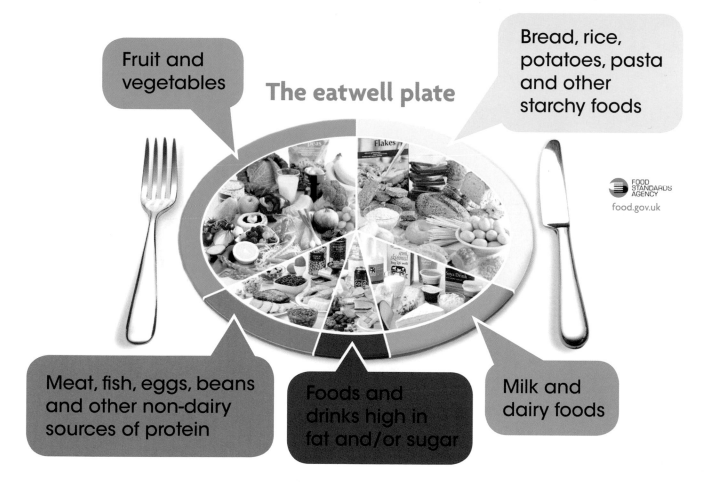

The eatwell plate shows the different sorts of food we can eat.

Different foods

You need to eat lots of different foods every day.

You need to eat lots of fruit
and vegetables.

You need to eat some protein.

Meat and fish have protein. Eggs,
nuts, and beans have protein, too.

You need to eat some dairy foods.

Dairy foods are made from milk.

You need to eat some grains.

Pasta, bread, and cereal are
made from grains.

whole grain

Foods made from whole grains
are best.

Grains give you energy.

Watch what you eat!

Some foods have a lot of fat.

Some foods have a lot of salt.

Some foods have a lot of sugar.

Do not have too much of these foods.

Keep trying

Even if you do not like something,
try to eat a little bit.

Don't be scared to try new things.

Food quiz

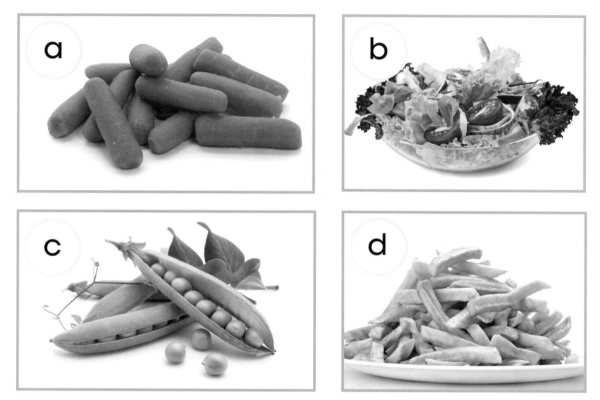

a

b

c

d

Which of these foods should you not eat too much of?

Answer on page 24

Picture glossary

 **dairy foods** food made from milk. Butter, cheese, and yoghurt are dairy foods.

 **energy** the power to do something. We need energy when we work or play.

 **grains** small, hard seed. Grains can be broken into parts. Wholegrain foods use all the parts and are better for us.

Index

The answer to the question on page 22 is d.
You should try not to eat a lot of chips because
they are high in fat.

Notes for parents and teachers

Before reading
Ask the children what it means to eat well. Explain that our bodies need a mixture of
different foods to stay healthy. Can they think of different foods we need? We also need
to limit the amount of foods that are high in fat, sugar, or salt in order to eat well. Can
the children think of many foods that are high in fat, sugar, or salt?

After reading
- Look at the eatwell plate on p5 together. Discuss the main food groups and how much
  food we should eat from each group. Potatoes are in the group with grains because
  they are another starchy food that gives us energy. The eatwell plate also shows which
  foods we should only eat a small amount of – can the children spot what these are?
- Discuss the importance of trying new foods and of trying small amounts of food they
  think they don't like. Explain that our tastes change as we get older and the more we
  try, the more we learn to like different foods. Challenge the children to keep a food
  diary for a week. A sticker chart could be used to record the new foods tried.